W9-CPI-788

People of Destiny

A Humanities Series

There comes a time,
we know not when,
that marks
the destiny of men.

Joseph Addison Alexander

People of Destiny

HARRY S. TRUMAN

By Kenneth G. Richards

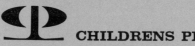

CHILDRENS PRESS, CHICAGO

*The editors wish to express
their appreciation to Mr. Meyer Goldberg,
who created the series and inspired
the publication of People of Destiny.*

Cover and body design: John Hollis

Project editor: Joan Downing

*Illustrations: Harley Shelton—Hollis
Associates*

Research editor: Robert Hendrickson

*Photographs: From the files of Wide World
Photos, Inc.*

Typesetting: American Typesetting Co.

Printing: Regensteiner Press

*Quotations on pages 11; 19; 22; 24, col. 1, ll. 12-15; 25; 26; 27;
30, col. 1; 30, col. 2, ll. 6-8; 32; 33; 39; 41; 49; 51; 55; 56; and
61 reprinted by permission of G. P. Putnam's Sons from THE
MAN FROM MISSOURI: THE LIFE AND TIMES OF
HARRY S. TRUMAN by Alfred Steinberg. Copyright © 1962
by Alfred Steinberg.*

*Quotations on pages 21; 24, col. 1, ll. 8-10; 30, col. 2, ll. 20-23;
and 47 from THIS MAN TRUMAN by Frank McNaughton
and Walter Hehmeyer. Copyright © 1945 by Frank McNaughton
and Walter Hehmeyer. Published by McGraw-Hill Book Company.*

*Library of Congress Catalog Card No. 68-15563
Copyright © 1968 by Regensteiner Publishing Enter-
prises, Inc. All rights reserved. Printed in the U.S.A.
Published simultaneously in Canada.*

2 3 4 5 6 7 8 9 10 11 12 13 14 15 16 17 18 19 20 21 22 23 24 25 R 75 74 73 72 71 70 69

Contents

A New Role for America

Thursday, April 12, 1945, was a cold, drizzly day in Washington, D.C. Cars, mostly military and government vehicles, splashed through standing puddles of water. The huge, needle-like Washington Monument stood stark and gray against a somber sky. The cherry trees, a prewar gift from Japan, cast misty bare-limbed reflections in the Tidal Basin near the Jefferson Memorial. Crowds of war workers bustled about in their effort to help win the war on the "home front." At the Capitol, Vice-President Harry S. Truman presided over a Senate discussion of a pending treaty with Mexico. President Franklin Delano Roosevelt, weary after his long journey to Russia for the Yalta Conference with Stalin and Churchill, was recuperating at his cottage in Warm Springs, Georgia.

On this April day, the end of World War II was not yet in sight—but there was no longer any doubt as to the outcome. Just the day before, American troops had punched through the German lines and reached the Elbe River near the ancient city of Magdeburg. Other American forces were driving relentlessly eastward through Germany. British and Canadian armies were slanting across Hitler's *Reich* toward Bremen and Hamburg. Huge Russian armies were poised for a final drive toward Berlin which would begin on the thirteenth.

In the Pacific Theater of Operations, General MacArthur had secured the Philippines, and the United States Marines had placed the Stars and Stripes on Iwo Jima's Mount Suribachi. On the first of April, the United States

Tenth Army had landed on Okinawa and now, eleven days later, was slugging it out with the Japanese defenders. Though casualties had been high at both Iwo Jima and Okinawa, they were said to be minor compared to the losses anticipated in the invasion of the Japanese home islands, scheduled for the fall. All these factors were on the minds of Americans as they went about their daily routine on that fateful Thursday in April, 1945.

It was a little after five in the afternoon when the Senate adjourned for the day and the Vice-President made his way to the southern end of the Capitol. He planned to stop in House Speaker Sam Rayburn's hideaway office which was jestingly known as Rayburn's "Board of Education." The Vice-President opened the door and was greeted warmly by Speaker Rayburn, Lewis Deschler, who was the parliamentarian of the House of Representatives, and James Barnes, a presidential executive assistant. Mr. Truman gave a cheery "Hello" and was about to make himself comfortable in a big leather chair when Speaker Rayburn stopped him.

"Steve Early called from the White House a couple of minutes ago, Harry," said Mr. Rayburn. "He sounded a little upset and asked that you call the White House as soon as you arrived."

Early was the White House press secretary.

Mr. Truman picked up the telephone and asked for the White House. He soon heard Early's voice on the other end of the line asking him to come right over.

The Vice-President sensed the urgency with which the Press Secretary spoke and assured Early that he would be right over. Then, his face pale, Mr. Truman hung up the phone and turned to the others in the room.

For a long few seconds the four men stared at each other in stunned silence. Then, regaining his composure, Mr. Truman said grimly, "Boys, this is in this room. Something must have happened. I'll be back soon." With that he strode quickly from the room, then went across the basement of the Capitol and through the underground tunnel to his office in the Senate Office Building. There he ordered his chauffeur to get the car ready. In his haste he had slipped away from his assigned Secret Service men and made the journey to the White House unguarded.

In a few moments the car swung into the circular drive at 1600 Pennsylvania Avenue. The Vice-President strode quickly through the great doors and into the White House lobby. He was ushered immediately to the elevator and then to Mrs. Roosevelt's second-floor study. It was evident from the faces of those in the room that something was indeed wrong. Mrs. Roosevelt stepped forward, put her arm gently on Mr. Truman's shoulder, and told him quietly that the President was dead.

For a moment, Mr. Truman was too stunned to speak. He had half expected that this was the news he would hear

Events of the fateful evening of April 12, 1945, the day President Roosevelt died, are depicted in the illustration: Truman's arrival at Rayburn's office, and the stunned staring of the men present there; the phone call to Steve Early, White House press secretary; the trip to the White House, and Mrs. Roosevelt's announcement that her husband had died, making Truman the president.

but the realization that his fears were true came as a blinding shock. Tears flooded his eyes as he struggled for words before at last he found his voice and asked whether there were anything he could do for her.

Mrs. Roosevelt asked whether she could help *him* in any way.

Later Mr. Truman recalled, how difficult it had been for him to grasp the fact that President Roosevelt had died. Though he had been afraid that this might happen, he found it hard to believe at the moment he was told.

With the passing of the initial shock, Mr. Truman took charge of the situation. First, he ordered that a government plane be made available to Mrs. Roosevelt for a flight to Warm Springs. Then he asked that all members of the Cabinet be called to a special meeting as quickly as possible. Next, he called Mrs. Truman and their daughter Margaret to tell them the sad news and to arrange for them to come to the White House.

At seven that evening about twenty people, mostly government officials and

members of Congress, gathered in the Cabinet Room. In contrast to the gala inauguration ceremonies usually accorded incoming presidents, the atmosphere was charged with grief and anxiety. Many of those in the crowded room were weeping openly as Chief Justice of the Supreme Court, Harlan Fiske Stone, administered the oath of office. Pale and grim-faced, the Vice-President placed his left hand on a Bible, raised his right hand and solemnly repeated the oath. The hands of the clock on the wall stood at exactly 7:09 when Harry S. Truman dropped his right hand and became the thirty-third president of the United States.

There were no rousing cheers on this occasion, no thunderous applause, no inaugural parade. But members of the

Without the usual fanfare accompanying this ritual, Harry S. Truman is sworn into office as the thirty-third president of the United States. The ceremony was performed by Chief Justice of the Supreme Court Harlan Fiske Stone. The illustration shows the flag at half-mast. It is flown this way for thirty days after the death of a president or former president.

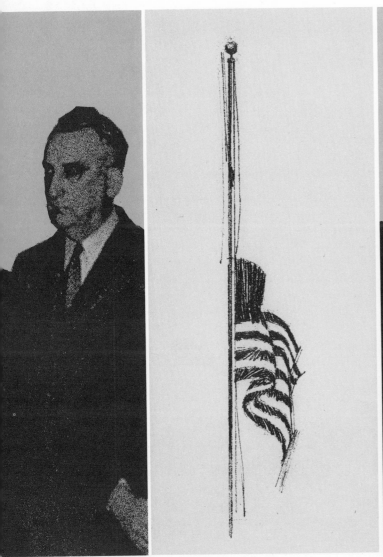

Congress and the Cabinet came forward to shake his hand, squeeze his arm, or pat his shoulder and offer the new President their full support for the trials ahead. They were aware of the awesome burden that had suddenly been thrust upon this man from Missouri. After a very brief Cabinet meeting, the new President went home to his apartment on Connecticut Ave.

President Harry S. Truman began his first full day as leader of the American people on Friday the thirteenth of April, 1945. To the superstitious, that date suggested bad luck. But Harry Truman was not a superstitious man. Nor did he suffer from a lack of self-confidence. He did, however, recognize the immense task before him.

Indeed, at this moment in American history, the office of president of the United States was becoming even more burdened with responsibility. A major shift of world power was occurring. The global burdens that England had borne for nearly a century were becoming America's responsibility. Henceforth, the president of the United States would, to a large extent, become the leader of the free world.

For a brief period, Harry Truman's main job would be to preside over the final defeat of the Axis powers. Even this required one of the most momentous decisions in history—to drop the atom bomb on Hiroshima and usher in the Atomic Age. Other than that, the final blueprint for victory had been drawn before he took office.

It was the postwar era that was to impose severe burdens upon the American president and his people. With the final defeat of the Axis, there emerged a new threat to the freedom and liberty of mankind—communism. It quickly became evident that this new attempt at world conquest must be challenged. The eyes of free men everywhere fell upon America for aid and protection. The isolationism which had for so long characterized American foreign policy had to be exchanged for global commitments to preserve freedom-loving nations. It would require a strong president to set the policy and establish a precedent for this new role America was to play in world history. America had such a man in Harry S. Truman.

In the years ahead, this man from Missouri would lead his nation and the free world in the containment of international communism. He would never waver, never vacillate, in his beliefs and principles. With the Truman Doctrine of aid to Greece and Turkey he demonstrated America's deep interest and concern for the security of smaller nations. With the Marshall Plan for European economic recovery, he proved America's concern for the welfare of mankind. With the Berlin Airlift, he emphasized American courage and integrity in the face of threats, and in Korea he proved that aggression anywhere in the world would be met with force. American policy and her place in the world were changed during Harry Truman's walk with destiny.

To Harry S. Truman, as president of the United States, fell the responsibility of presiding over the defeat of the Axis powers and ending World War II. Though most of the groundwork for the plan of attack had already been done, Truman had to make the major decision of whether or not to drop the atom bomb on Japan.

A Horseshoe for Luck

Lamar is a quiet village on the northern edge of the Ozarks in western Missouri. In 1884, it was a farm community with a population of about 800. Its streets were rutted by the wheels of wagons and it was not unusual to see livestock driven through the town. Lamar's chief distinction was that Wyatt Earp had served as the town constable before moving west to greater fame. On May 8, 1884, however, an event took place in Lamar which six decades later would be of great significance to the United States and to the world. In a low, white frame house which had no number, standing on a little dirt street which had no name, the thirty-third President of the United States was born.

The baby's parents were John and Martha Truman, both native Missourians, who had grown up together on neighboring farms in Grandview, near Kansas City. John Anderson Truman's ancestry was English. His family had migrated to Connecticut in 1666 and later to Kentucky before moving west to Missouri in the 1840's.

Martha Ellen Young was of German extraction. Her father, Solomon, was a wagon master for the pioneers heading to the unsettled West in the years before and during the American Civil War. Solomon was often gone for months at a time as he guided the great Conestoga wagon trains across the plains to Utah and then over the Rocky Mountains to California. His business prospered and Solomon invested in land and farms. His wife Harriet looked after the farms and kept affairs in order during his absence.

Harry Truman's parents, John and Martha Truman, on their wedding day in 1882. They had known each other since childhood, when they lived on neighboring farms in Grandview, Missouri, near Kansas City.

Missouri, a border state, was divided in its allegiance during the Civil War. No major battles were fought there, but the state bled and suffered as brother fought against brother and good neighbors became bitter enemies. The Young family sympathized with the Confederates and consequently suffered at the hands of Unionists and the Union Army. One day the infamous guerrilla leader, Jim Lane, rode up to the Young farm and forced Grandmother Young to cook for his band of Kansas renegades. Then they stole all they could carry, shot all the livestock, and moved on.

The climax of the bloody guerrilla fighting in the Kansas–Missouri area came on August 20, 1863, when the Confederate raider, William Quantrill, sacked and burned Lawrenceville, Kansas. Union General Ewing then issued an order to all Confederates in several Missouri counties to leave their homes. Martha Ellen Young, eleven years old, trudged into exile behind an oxcart loaded with a few family possessions. The coming of peace in 1865 could not erase the bitterness many farmers of western Missouri felt for the Union.

But the Civil War had been over for nearly twenty years when Harry Truman was born. By 1884, the lawlessness that had followed the Civil War was also ending. Guerrilla warfare had continued for awhile in Missouri and the Midwest, and this was followed by the banditry of the James and Dalton gangs. Eventually the lawbreakers were rounded up, however, and in 1882 Jesse James was killed in St. Joseph, Missouri. The state prospered during

Missouri was plagued with guerrilla fighting during the Civil War. This illustration shows the burning of Lawrenceville, Kansas, Martha Ellen Young's childhood home, by William Quantrill, a Confederate raider.

the years before Harry's birth in 1884, and the Trumans and Youngs also prospered.

John Truman had brought his bride to Lamar in 1882 where he established a business as a horse and mule trader. The little farm soon became a center where the menfolk of the community gathered to talk politics, "swap yarns," and "dicker" on animal trades and sales. John Truman was a short man and all his life answered to the nickname "Peanuts." He was a pleasant and popular man but despite his size and good nature could show a violent temper when he was aroused. These characteristics would later become evident in his eldest son.

Martha Truman was a tiny, vivacious girl with dark hair and laughing eyes. Martha's small size was misleading. She was an outdoor girl who loved horses and was an accomplished rider. She spoke in a firm decisive manner that would someday become a trademark of her son.

Finding a name for their son proved to be a controversial issue in the family. "I was supposed to be named Harrison Shippe Truman, taking my middle name from my paternal grandfather," Harry explained later. "Others in the family wanted my middle name to be Solomon, taken from my maternal grandfather. But apparently no agreement could be reached and my name was recorded and stands simply as Harry S. Truman." And so the "S" stands for nothing and the "Harrison" (Martha's oldest brother's name) was shortened to "Harry." Despite the trouble in choosing a name, John was

so elated at the birth of his first son that he nailed a horseshoe over the front door to bring his boy good luck.

Harry was only a year old when his father moved the family to Harrisonville. It was here that Harry's brother John Vivian was born on April 25, 1886. Business was no better in Harrisonville that it had been in Lamar, and in 1887, John Truman moved his family once again. They moved in with Martha's folks, the Youngs, at Grandview.

Grandfather Young's house was a rambling eight-room, two-story home which was painted white as were the two barns, huge granary, and half-dozen hog sheds. Harry Truman's life really began here, for his earliest memories were of this farm. He lived here for nearly four happy years, spending his days following the grown-ups around as they did their chores on the farm. Harry's sister Mary Jane was born here in August of 1889.

Harry was anything but a spoiled child. His mother was a firm disciplinarian who kept a little switch handy. The future President got his share of lickings. "We were taught," he remembered years later, "that punishment always followed transgression, and my mother saw to it that it did." John Truman, despite his temper, never spanked his children. But his scoldings, Harry would recall, "hurt worse than a good spanking."

With the birth of Mary Jane, there were now five Trumans living in the old farmhouse with the Youngs, plus servants, farmhands, and several other relatives. John Truman decided that it was time once more to strike out on his own. With a small inheritance received upon the death of his father, John bought a house and barn on a good-sized lot in the town of Independence in Jackson County.

Independence was already an historic town. During the years before the Civil War, it had been the only town of consequence west of St. Louis. For years it had been the jumping-off point for the Santa Fe and Oregon trails—the last bit of civilization for the thousands of pioneers heading west. It had also served as a sanctuary for the much-persecuted Mormons before mobs drove them away in the 1830's.

When the Truman family moved there in 1890, the town boasted a population of about 6000 and was a bustling community. Old-timers remembered the past fame of the little city and many tales were recited at the Truman horse-trading business on Chrysler Street. None could realize then, of course, that the six-year-old boy who helped his father with the horses would someday bring new fame to Independence. None could suspect that John Truman's little boy Harry would become the thirty-third president of the United States.

Left, Harry S. Truman's birthplace in Lamar, Missouri, as it looked in 1944. The owner of the house at that time, eighty-six-year-old W.M. Earp (center) points to the window of the room in which Truman was born. Below, wagons are shown leaving the town of Independence, Missouri, where John Truman moved his family in 1890. Before the Civil War, Independence had been the last major town before the beginning of the Santa Fe and Oregon trails across the Great Plains.

21

The Youthful Mediator

The boy who came to Independence in 1890 was already a studious lad. He could read parts of the Bible even before he was six years old. In fact, at a very young age, he could quote many verses at random. His mother discovered, however, that young Harry had difficulty reading the small print in the Bible. It was soon obvious that something was wrong with Harry's eyes.

At last the concerned mother took the boy to an oculist in Kansas City. An extensive examination confirmed her fears—his eyes were very poor. A prescription was made and Harry Truman began wearing the thick-lensed glasses that he still requires.

Not long after his arrival in Independence, Harry began attending Sunday school at the First Presbyterian Church. Though his parents were Baptists, the Presbyterian minister had welcomed the family so warmly

that the Truman children were sent to his church. It was at this Sunday school that Harry first met a lovely little golden-haired girl who was only a year younger than he. Her name was Elizabeth Virginia Wallace, though everyone called her "Bess." In later years, Harry remembered their first meeting and said, "I was too backward to look at her very much. And I didn't speak to her for five years." This first encounter was, however, the beginning of a relationship which would blossom into a lifetime romance in the years ahead.

Harry was past his eighth birthday before he entered school. From the very first he proved to be a good student. Because he was somewhat frail physically, and especially because of his poor eyesight, Harry did not participate in school sports such as hockey, football, or baseball. He was popular with his

The illustration shows Harry Truman meeting Bess Wallace at the First Presbyterian Church in Independence, where they both attended Sunday school. Many years later, Bess Wallace was to become the wife of Harry S. Truman.

schoolmates, however, and was frequently called upon to umpire at games.

Because he could not participate in sports, Harry spent many hours at the Independence Public Library. He had a sharp and accurate memory and he seemed to accumulate facts and figures with amazing ease. "I had more useless information floating around in my head than any man," he has said with a grin. He especially loved histories and biographies of famous people. "I read everything I could get my hands on," he reported, "histories and encyclopedias and everything else." He had read the Bible through twice before he was twelve.

Harry was also accident prone. Once he fell off a chair and broke his collarbone. Another time he nearly choked to death on a peach stone and only the quick action of his mother in forcing the pit down his throat saved his life. He sliced off the tip of his big toe by slamming a door on it. With all this, besides the usual knocks and bruises a boy receives, it is a wonder Harry survived.

He had a near fatal case of diphtheria, a disease that swept through the family in 1893. His younger brother, Vivian, contracted the disease but recovered quickly. Harry was left with partly paralyzed arms and legs, and it was several months before he returned to good health.

When he was about ten years old, Harry began taking piano lessons, first with his mother and then with Mrs. E. C. White of Kansas City. The Trumans had an old upright piano in the parlor and each morning Harry would arise at five o'clock and put in two hours of practice before school. He was a diligent, if not gifted, student, and both his mother and teacher were pleased with his progress.

The Harry Truman of grammar school days was a quiet, somewhat shy boy, good-natured, and had a ready smile. In all his school days, he never had a fistfight. In fact, he became the media-

Here we see young Harry Truman at the old upright piano in the Trumans' parlor, faithfully practicing his lessons before school.

tor for spats and clashes among other students. The other boys came to respect the bespectacled lad for his common sense and sincerity. He had a knack for reconciling disputes and restoring peace on the playground. Once he had weighed the problem and arrived at a decision, he stood firm for the position he believed was right.

Like most brothers, Harry and Vivian had their share of squabbles and quarrels, but neither fought with other boys. The two brothers were opposites in many respects. Harry was the scholarly type, Vivian a rugged outdoorsman. Harry enjoyed playing the piano, Vivian would have none of it. "Mama couldn't get a lasso big enough," he recalled in later years.

Harry was especially fond of his little sister, Mary Jane, who was five years his junior. When she was tiny, he often rocked her to sleep and sang to her at bedtime. When she grew older he watched over her outdoors, and some mornings before school even braided her hair. He was a very attentive brother. Years later, Mary Jane recalled, "Harry used to take me everywhere. Perhaps that's why I'm an old maid, because he was such a nice beau."

In 1896, John Truman sold the house on Chrysler Street and moved to Waldo Street where Harry was accepted as a sort of part-time member of the "Waldo Street Gang." It was a happy-go-lucky neighborhood, and the "gang" always had something to do for fun. There was a pond nearby where they swam in the summer and skated in the winter. They fished on the banks of the Missouri River and the Little Blue. And for Harry, the "gang" held another attraction—one member was a golden-haired tomboy by the name of Bess Wallace. Harry later remembered the wonderful times he had in that neighborhood during the years he lived there.

Despite his late start in school, Harry advanced quickly through his classes and had soon caught up with his own age group. In high school, his favorite subjects were Latin and history. With his pals, Charley Ross and Elmer Twy-man, Harry worked for several weeks on a special project in which they took great pride. Most boys of those days were accomplished with pocketknives, and this trio put their talents to good use. Together they whittled an exactly scaled replica of one of the bridges Caesar had built across the Rhine. They had found a description of the bridge in Caesar's *Commentaries*.

In the spring of 1898, the United States went to war with Spain following the sinking of the battleship *Maine* in Havana Harbor. A wave of patriotism swept the country as the slogan "Remember the *Maine*!" called Americans to their duty. Lieutenant Colonel Theodore Roosevelt organized his "Rough Riders" for an invasion of Spanish-held Cuba and Commodore George Dewey devastated the Spanish Asiatic fleet at Manila Bay.

Back in Independence, Missouri, Harry Truman and the Waldo Street Gang organized the Independence Junior Militia. They held weekly drills with .22-caliber rifles, occasionally shooting a barnyard fowl or two to take

along on their "bivouacs" beside the Little Blue River. "There were a dozen or more of us," Harry remembered later with a grin. "We liked to think we would join the armed forces as a unit if the Spanish-American War would only wait for us to get old enough." The war ended in effect, however, with the destruction of the Spanish fleet by Admiral Sampson at Santiago, Cuba, on July 3, 1898. And so the Junior Militia returned to school that fall, their dreams of glory and valor on the battlefield dashed by the Spanish surrender. Most would get their chance two decades later in the terrible trench warfare on the fields of France.

In the fall of that year, 1898, Harry took his first job. He helped out before and after school at Jim Clinton's drugstore on a corner of the town square. The pay was only three dollars per week and Harry had to report for work at six-thirty every morning. He swept the sidewalk, mopped the floors, washed windows, dusted bottles and display cases, and performed a dozen other tasks. But one of Harry's outstanding charac-

teristics was that of being a hard and willing worker, and he never complained.

Harry Truman graduated from high school with the class of 1901. He was now seventeen and eagerly looked forward to continued schooling—possibly at the University of Missouri. Soon after Harry's graduation, however, John Truman suffered financial losses. It was soon apparent that there would be little money left with which to send Harry to college. In fact, the Trumans had to sell their Waldo Street home and buy a small place in nearby Kansas City. Harry thought of working his way through college, but instead had to get a job in order to help John Vivian and Mary Jane stay in school. The future did not look very bright.

Almost overnight, Harry Truman had become a man with responsibilities to his family. Ahead lay long years of frustrations, heartbreak, and occasional failures. But all the experiences ahead would serve to mold the character and develop the traits with which, at a later day, Harry Truman would confidently meet his moment of destiny.

The Farmer from Grandview

Harry Truman's first full-time job was as a timekeeper for a railroad contractor named L. J. Smith. This six-day-a-week job thrust the quiet-spoken, bespectacled young man into a world he had never seen. Some of the horse and mule traders who had done business with his father were rough-hewn characters. But the 400-odd "gandy dancers," or railroad hoboes, who were laying track for L. J. Smith were the rabble of the earth.

Harry's job was to make out the timecards for the men who worked in three crews. Twice daily he pumped a handcar between the camps, ate with the hoboes from tin pans, and lived in the dirty tents with the most profane men he had ever known. Every other Saturday night, Harry had to sign paychecks for the men, usually in a back room of some bar either in Independence or Sheffield. These men would cash the checks at the bar and drink their earnings away before arriving back at work on Monday morning. In June of 1902, Harry left his job and went in search of new work. He had

Railroad hoboes, or "gandy dancers," were often hired to lay railroad track, and as his first job, Harry worked for a contractor named L.J. Smith, making out timecards for these men. Here we see the gandy dancers at work on a new stretch of track.

had enough of the gandy dancers, though the job had been good experience. He had learned how to handle rough, tough, uneducated men and make them respect him.

By now John Vivian was out of school and the two Truman boys took jobs with the National Bank of Commerce in Kansas City. Harry worked in the "zoo," or caged area in the basement of the bank. It was dull work and he complained to a friend, "I don't have enough responsibility. I don't have anything to decide." As if the monotony were not bad enough, there seemed to be no hope of getting ahead. "The vice-president would always remember a trivial mistake when a clerk asked for a raise," he complained. In 1904, Harry quit his job and accepted a position with the Union National Bank as a bookkeeper at a twenty-five-dollar per month increase in salary.

Meanwhile, John Truman had traded his small Kansas City house for a down payment on a farm near Clinton, some sixty miles to the southeast. Harry moved into Mrs. Trow's boardinghouse where he paid five dollars a week for a room and two meals a day. One of his fellow roomers was a young man named Arthur Eisenhower from Abilene, Kansas, who spoke often of his younger brother Dwight.

On Saturday afternoons, Harry worked as an usher at the Grand Theater where he got a free view of such popular performers as Lillian Russell, Eva Tanguay, and the Four Cohans. Now and then he would treat himself to a classical concert; at one of these he came to admire Josef Lhevinne, the pianist. On another memorable occasion, he ran from the bank to Tenth and Main streets to catch a glimpse of President Theodore Roosevelt. He remembers being a little disappointed that Roosevelt "was no giant, but a little man in a long Prince Albert coat to make him look taller."

On Flag Day in 1905, Harry became a charter member of the newly formed Battery B of the Missouri National Guard. The battery drilled once a week at the armory and held field maneuvers on weekends. Private Truman served on a 3-inch light gun. He was very proud of his blue uniform but the first time he wore it home was the last time. Grandmother Young, still remembering the tragedy of bygone days, told him firmly, "Harry! This is the first time a uniform of that color has been in this house since the Civil War. Don't bring it back!"

In the fall of 1905, John Truman suffered another loss. This time floods had ruined his entire crop of corn on the Clinton farm. In October, he and Martha moved back to the Young farm at Grandview. Harry's Uncle Harrison had been managing the farm, but decided to move to the city. The 600-acre farm was too much for the elder Truman, and he asked Harry and Vivian to return and help. In the early summer of 1906, Harry left Kansas City behind and took on the hard work and long hours of a farmer.

It was in this same year, 1906, that Harry Truman got his start in politics. His father had become active in the Pendergast machine, a political organization which exerted considerable in-

The illustration shows Harry looking eagerly at President Theodore Roosevelt as the President passed through Kansas City.

fluence in Kansas City. As a reward for services on behalf of this Democratic machine, John Truman was appointed an elections judge in the Grandview precinct. Harry became his clerk and thus took his first tentative step into the world of politics.

Running a large farm was hard work, but Harry Truman proved to be a good farmer. During the summer months, he arose at four-thirty every morning and "plowed, sowed, reaped, milked cows, fed hogs, doctored horses, baled hay, and did everything there was to do on a 600-acre farm." Many neighbors looked askance at Harry's farming methods, for he used a business-like approach. He increased productivity by rotating crops. He understood soil conservation. He maintained records of

costs-per-acre of his various crops and he invested in modern equipment.

Despite the hard work on the farm, Harry Truman still had to find other outlets for his bubbling energy. He became a member of the Beltown Masonic Lodge and later organized a lodge in Grandview. He also helped organize the Jackson County Farm Bureau.

In the meantime, he had found still another interest in life—Miss Bess Wallace, the little girl he had so admired many years before. Bess' family was fairly well-to-do, and the vivacious girl enjoyed a pleasant homelife with her widowed mother and her grandparents.

In 1913, Harry purchased a secondhand Stafford touring car to ease the travel problem involved in courting a girl who lived so far away. The Stafford

was a fine automobile in its day and made quite an impression on Bess' family. Her brothers, George and Frank, and their girl friends used to pile in, along with Harry and Bess, for country rides and picnics. These were happy years for farmer Harry Truman.

In 1914, the year World War I exploded upon the world, tragedy also struck the Trumans of Grandview. John Truman had suffered an intestinal block during the summer and underwent surgery at a Kansas City hospital. He returned home to recuperate and seemed to be on the mend when he died quietly in his sleep one November evening. Harry later told of that fateful night. "I had been sitting with him and watching a long time," he said. "I fell asleep for a short time and when I woke up he was dead." John Truman would never know the future awaiting his son.

At the time of his death, John Truman held a political appointment as road overseer in the Eastern District of Jackson County. Besides bossing a crew which repaired roads, bridges, and culverts in the area, Truman had also

In 1913, Harry purchased a secondhand touring car. In it, he could easily travel to see Bess. Harry, Bess, and Bess' brothers and their girl friends all spent many pleasant hours going for drives and picnicking in the country.

33

This illustration shows the men of Morgan and Company drilling for oil in test wells. Harry S. Truman invested a large sum of money in this company and was its treasurer. No oil was ever found in its wells.

served as a local representative for the Pendergast political machine. Harry, who had been attending weekly meetings of the Kansas City Tenth Ward Democratic Club, was given his father's old post as road overseer. A year later, in 1915, he was appointed postmaster of Grandview, a job which paid fifty dollars a month. Harry turned his entire paycheck over to his assistant.

It was in 1915 also that Harry took a fling in the mining business. With an investment of $2000, he became part owner of a mine at Commerce, Oklahoma. Since the outbreak of the European war, there had been a great demand for lead and zinc. Harry had high hopes of striking it rich. But no metal was found, and Harry lost his $2000.

In 1916, Harry borrowed $5000 to invest in an oil business called Morgan and Company. Harry became its treasurer and soon developed a great interest in the oil business. Bad luck dogged the company, however, and while it made money in lease manipulations on property, no oil was ever discovered in its test wells.

Meanwhile, America was drawing closer and closer to the war in Europe. Germany's resumption of unrestricted submarine warfare brought about a break in diplomatic relations between that country and America in February of 1917. It was now only a matter of time before the American people would demand a declaration of war against the Central Powers of Europe. On April 6, 1917, the declaration of war was made and American doughboys were soon on their way "over there."

Harry had resigned from the National Guard in 1911. Now that his country called, however, he was among the first to offer his services. Within a year, Harry Truman was to find himself on the soil of France leading a battery of field artillery in the battles on the western front. It was here that the leadership qualities which would be so sorely needed in future years were first discovered in the man who came to be known as "Captain Harry of Battery D."

Captain Harry of Battery D

Soon after America entered World War I, plans were made to create the Second Missouri Field Artillery. The nucleus for the six-battery force was to be Battery C of Independence and Harry's old outfit, Battery B of Kansas City. Leaving the farm in the hands of his sister, Mary Jane, Harry immediately began a recruiting campaign to help build the Second to its required strength. A wave of patriotism was sweeping the country and recruiting was not difficult for Harry, who was the most enthusiastic patriot of all.

In World War I, as in previous American wars, the enlisted men elected their company officers—both commissioned and noncoms. Because of his past National Guard experience, Harry was secretly hoping to be elected a section sergeant. The men paid him an even greater compliment. When the votes were tallied, Harry had been elected a first lieutenant. On August 5, 1917, the Second Missouri Field Artillery was sworn into the regular army as a unit and became the One Hundred and Twenty-ninth Artillery of the United States Thirty-fifth Division. First Lieutenant Harry Truman was attached to Battery F.

In September, the One Hundred and Twenty-ninth left Kansas City for training at Fort Sill, Oklahoma. Here, he and another officer, Eddie Jacobson, were given the job of opening and managing a canteen—the equivalent of today's post exchange. This, of course,

---

During World War I, Harry helped recruit men for the Second Missouri Field Artillery. He is shown here in his United States Army uniform after his fellow soldiers elected him a first lieutenant. His company was sworn into the army as a unit, and was called the One Hundred and Twenty-ninth Artillery.

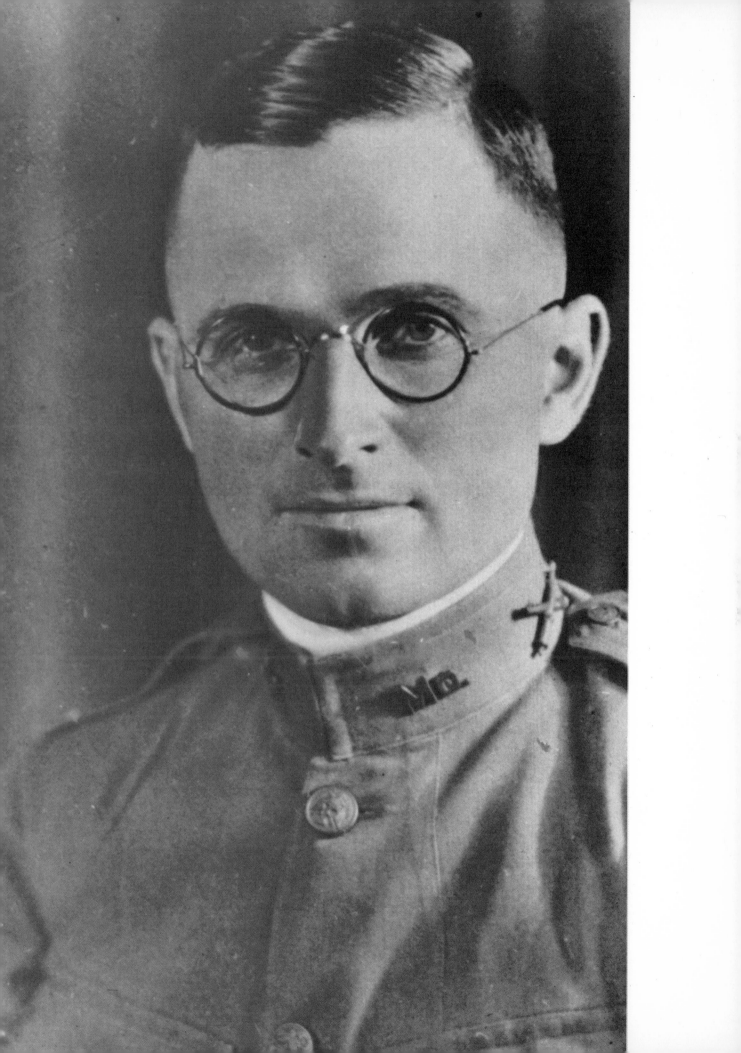

was in addition to his normal military duties as an artillery officer. Both officers proved to be good businessmen and theirs was the only canteen at Fort Sill to show a profit.

The months passed quickly for the unit as the men were kept busy learning all the finer points of army life—especially learning to be first-rate artillerymen. In March of 1918, Harry, nine other officers, and one hundred enlisted men were selected to go to France for specialized training. The rest of the unit would follow later. On the way across the country by train, Harry persuaded a railroad man in a small Kansas town to let him use the company telephone to call Bess. By this time, Harry and Bess were unofficially engaged. Despite the early hour—it was four in the morning—Bess was thrilled to talk with Harry before he went overseas.

Harry and the advance party from the One Hundred and Twenty-ninth arrived in Brest aboard the *George Washington* on April 13, 1918. From there they were sent to a special artillery school at Montigne-sur-Aube where they were trained in the firing of the big French .75's. After five weeks of intensive training, Harry rejoined the One Hundred and Twenty Ninth. The unit had now arrived in France and was stationed at a place called Camp Coetquidan—where Napoleon once had an artillery base.

By now Harry had been promoted to captain and on July 11, 1918, was given command of his own four-gun battery—the infamous Battery D, scourge of the unit. There were 188 men in Battery D (often referred to as "Dizzy D"), and most of them were rough, hard-boiled Irishmen from a tough neighborhood of Kansas City.

They had already run through three commanding officers, causing one a nervous breakdown, before Colonel Klemm ordered Harry to take over.

The big, boisterous artillerymen from Kansas City, who enjoyed their reputation of being unmanageable, grinned as the quiet, bespectacled Truman made his appearance that first morning. Nudging each other with their elbows, they whispered out of the corners of their mouths, "This one'll be easy!" and "We'll get rid of this guy in a hurry!"

As for Captain Truman, he remembered later: "I was the most thoroughly scared individual in that camp. Never on the front or anywhere else have I been so nervous."

Later that day, the men made their first attempt to embarrass their new CO. The battery had some 160 horses and, after waiting for Captain Truman to happen along, the men staged a mock stampede. This they felt sure would frighten the mild-mannered officer out of his wits. But Harry Truman had grown up around cattle and horses and he could tell at a glance that the "stampede" was faked. Instead of panicking as they had hoped, Harry just sat quietly on his horse and, with a complete lack of expression, watched the goings-on.

The hard-boiled Irishmen of Battery D enjoyed a reputation of being unmanageable, and tried to embarrass Captain Truman by staging a mock stampede. They hoped that their new commanding officer would panic, but instead he calmly sat on his horse and waited for the stampede to end.

39

Truman stopped his men from fleeing in panic from the Germans during "The Battle of Who Run" by shouting at them the curses he had learned during his work with the gandy dancers.

When the men had worn themselves out and stood sweating and dust covered with disgust and frustration showing on their faces, Harry ambled his horse toward the largest group of men. Seated calmly in his saddle, unruffled and unperturbed, he quietly ordered the men to clean up the debris, care for the horses, mend the harnesses, and repair the wagons. Then he rode quietly away as 180 swearing, sweating, toiling men labored to undo the mess they had created. It was quite a price to pay for a joke that had backfired.

That night, still smarting from their defeat, the men got into a free-for-all among themselves. They smashed cots, tore tents, shattered chairs, and sent four men to the infirmary. When Captain Truman heard of this the next morning, he called all the noncoms—the sergeants and corporals—into his office. Most entered with a grin, for they fully expected the new CO to plead for help, to whimper for their support, and to grant concessions in return for making the men behave. But their smirks faded quickly as Captain Truman rose steely-eyed behind his desk, and in a quiet voice which expressed as much in tone as it did in words, delivered instead of a plea, an ultimatum.

"You noncoms are responsible for maintaining discipline within your squads and sections," he reminded them. "I intend to see that this is done. Furthermore, I intend to bust any man back to private who can't do the job. If you want to keep those stripes on your arm, you'll have to prove to me that you merit them. Is that understood?"

With a few strangled "Yessirs" and "Yes Sir, Captain!" the noncoms filed out of the room convinced that the new CO meant business. The Dizzy D would never be a model battery as far as discipline was concerned. But under the command of the man they quickly came to respect and would eventually grow to love, Battery D would take a backseat to no one as a fighting unit.

It was the sixth of September before the One Hundred and Twenty-ninth saw any action. They had been assigned to a fairly quiet sector in the Vosges Mountains of Alsace. On this night there occurred what became known to Dizzy D as "The Battle of Who Run."

The "battle" began with a 500-round barrage fired at the German lines by Battery D. For a little while after the barrage, things were quiet; then suddenly the Germans retaliated in kind. With the first few shells to land near Battery D, which had never been under fire before, somebody panicked and suddenly almost every member of the unit was racing for his life. Captain Truman tried to rally his men, but to no avail. Then, livid with anger, Harry decided on one final attempt at turning the tide. Recalling the language of the gandy dancers on the railroad back in Missouri, Captain Truman began to curse. As his men streamed toward the rear, he stood amid the bursting German shells and screamed every blistering oath at them that he had ever heard. The regimental chaplain, Father Tiernan, said Harry turned the air blue. "It took the skin off the ears of those boys," he recalled later with a grin. "And it turned those boys right around."

The sight of their mild-mannered CO exploding into a tornado of unparalleled fury and wrath caused the men to stop and stare in wonderment. Then the basic courage of the brawling, fighting Irish overcame their first flashes of panic. If Captain Truman could do it, so could they. The men returned and at Harry's commands hitched up the guns and withdrew in orderly fashion some few hundred yards to safety.

After "Who Run," the men of Dizzy D had even greater respect and admiration for their usually quiet-spoken CO. Certainly none was ready to stir Captain Truman to the volcanic fury they had witnessed in their first action. Here was a real man—one who would

One night on the Meuse–Argonne front, in September of 1918, Captain Harry Truman crept forward to a vantage point from which he could view German positions. He had with him a field telephone with which he could call firing data to his Battery D, positioned in an apple orchard to the rear. Scanning the German lines with field glasses, he suddenly stopped and focused on a movement off to the right. Careful scrutiny revealed a German force moving around the American flank for a surprise attack on unsuspecting doughboy positions.

There were strict orders in effect to fire only in designated sectors. These Germans were not in Captain Truman's sector. Something had to be done, however, or the enemy would soon be overrunning American positions. There was no time to report this situation to headquarters and there was no time to request permission to fire out of his own sector. Captain Truman decided to risk a court-martial and take matters into his own hands.

Quickly calculating range and bearing, he telephoned his battery to meet this sneak threat. Battery D men leaped to their posts, fired a couple of rounds to zero in, and then laid a barrage of shells squarely on the Germans. In a few minutes, Captain Truman called, "Cease Fire!" and when the dust had cleared, it was revealed that one German battery had been destroyed and two others knocked out of commission. Battery D's quick action had saved many American lives.

The regimental historian later wrote of this incident. "How many men of the infantry, digging in on the open hillsides overhanging Charpentry and Baulny, owe their lives to the alertness, initiative, and efficiency of Captain Truman and to the quick responsiveness and trained efficiency of his men at the guns!"

wade in mud and put his shoulder to a caisson wheel along with the rest of them, one who demanded unquestioning obedience to orders but who had a deep personal concern for each of his men. This was a man who was genuine. This was a man who was strict but fair. This was "Captain Harry."

A week after "Who Run," the One Hundred and Twenty-ninth became a reserve unit of the first all-American offensive of the war—the Battle of the St. Mihiel Salient. General Douglas MacArthur achieved lasting fame in this action with his Forty-second Rainbow Division.

Shortly after midnight on September 26, 1918, the last great offensive of the war began on the Meuse-Argonne front and Battery D and the One Hundred and Twenty-ninth covered themselves with glory. Dizzy D members made up for their showing at "Who Run" by maintaining a hot and accurate fire at their targets. Captain Truman earned even more respect from the fighting Irish under his command, for he frequently reconnoitered alone—far ahead of the guns. He would telephone the location of enemy positions back to his men and then serve as a "spotter" to make sure their shells landed on target.

For mile after muddy mile the One Hundred and Twenty-ninth followed the retreating Germans. It was a wearying, back-breaking grind of unhitching the guns, firing several hundred rounds, hitching up, slogging through mud and mire for several hundred more yards, and digging in to fire again. On and on the offensive went, without letup, without respite, through October and into November. November 11 found the One Hundred and Twenty-ninth near the gutted city of Verdun. At five o'clock that morning word was passed that a cease-fire would become effective at eleven. At ten forty-five, Dizzy D fired its final shell and a few minutes later, peace descended upon the torn and shattered fields of France. World War I was over.

Two photographs of the fighting in World War I. Above, artillery in Europe. Truman's Battery D carried heavy guns much like these. Below, American infantry advancing through a forest, also somewhere in Europe.

The One Hundred and Twenty-ninth stayed in France until April of the following year. On Easter Sunday, April 20, 1919, the liner *Zeppelin* docked in New York and Captain Harry Truman and his men were home once more.

Colonel Klemm, the commanding officer of the One Hundred and Twenty-ninth, did not believe in handing out medals as many other officers did. Captain Truman explained his military career by saying, "I didn't do anything out of the ordinary. I was not wounded, and I got no citations of any kind." But he was honored in a way that was perhaps more meaningful than a government citation. In New York the men of the Dizzy D chipped in and purchased a silver loving cup which they presented to him as a token of their respect and esteem. It was engraved, "To Captain Harry from Battery D."

Colonel Klemm did recommend Truman for his majority, but before the promotion came through, Harry was out of the regular army. He became a major in the reserve corps.

Two days before his thirty-fifth birthday, Harry Truman became a civilian once more. Behind him lay nineteen months of service to his country, during which he came to realize his ability as a leader of men. He felt he could not return to the farm. A new ambition burned within him. There was yet to be a period of searching—a time of trial and frustration. But in time he would come to a crossroads and decide to take a path that would change the shape of his future.

Captain Harry Truman is circled in this group photograph of the men of Battery D, One Hundred and Twenty-ninth Artillery, taken in 1919 at Camp Mills, New York. The unit had just returned from overseas.

Rising Politician

The most important thing in Harry Truman's mind as he returned to civilian life was his coming marriage to Bess Wallace. She had prayed and worried during those months before the Armistice, knowing that Harry was in the thick of action. Now he was safely home and the happy couple began making wedding plans in earnest.

At last the day arrived—June 28, 1919. The ceremony was performed in Trinity Episcopal Church in Independence. It was a quiet, simple wedding, though the church was crowded to capacity with townspeople and almost the entire force of Battery D. Few of the ex-artillerymen missed the chance to attend the wedding of Captain Harry. Following a reception at the Gates–Wallace home at 219 North Delaware Street, the newlyweds left for a brief honeymoon in Chicago and Detroit.

When they returned, Harry and Bess moved into the big house with Grandmother Gates and the bride's mother, Mrs. Madge Wallace. This handsome old home, built in the 1880's, had fourteen rooms, three fireplaces, and was furnished with lovely antique furniture. This was a far more elegant place than Harry had ever lived in before.

With a wife to support, Harry set out to find a means of livelihood. He had already decided that he would not return to farming. One day in July he chanced to meet his partner of Fort Sill canteen days, Eddie Jacobson. As the two began reminiscing about old army days, Harry said, "Maybe we ought to go into business together and have a partnership again." Eddie liked the idea and the two ex-army buddies began discussing possibilities. At last they decided to set up a sort of civilian canteen—a men's furnishings store.

Pooling all the resources each could get his hands on, Truman & Jacobson opened their doors on November 29, 1919, with approximately $35,000 worth of men's shirts, socks, hats, underwear, and suits. Word got around quickly and soon the store was a gathering place for most of old Battery D. Times were good and the men made many purchases from their wartime CO.

Harry and Eddie worked hard at their business. Eddie was the buyer for the firm, and Harry the bookkeeper. They both did the selling. It was a six-day-a-week job, from eight in the morning until nine at night plus extra hours for taking inventories of stock or checking the books. Harry and Bess

Truman is shown in the men's furnishings store in Kansas City which he operated with his friend Eddie Jacobson from 1919 to 1922. Left to right: Truman; Francis Berry, who served in Battery D; Mike Flynn, a lieutenant in Battery D.

had only Sundays together, and this day they frequently spent visiting Harry's mother and sister in Grandview.

In 1921, a depression hit the country —not as severe as the "crash" which was to strike the country eight years later, but a depression, nevertheless. Farm prices fell, starting a chain reaction in the price of other goods. The Truman & Jacobson store was forced to cut its prices bit by bit until finally their margin of profit was gone. Meanwhile creditors were demanding payment. In 1922 the partnership failed and the business closed its doors. Harry refused to file a petition of bankruptcy and, instead, was to spend the next fifteen years paying his share of the debts.

The failure of the clothing business, though a major tragedy for Harry Truman at the time, indirectly led him into the field of politics. Had the business prospered, it is doubtful that Harry S. Truman would ever have become the thirty-third president of the United States. When the business collapsed, however, he began casting about for a new means of livelihood. Since he had always had an interest in politics, it is not surprising that he turned to this profession.

To be elected to almost any post in Jackson County required the backing of one of the political "machines." Harry had attended party meetings in the past. He also was a friend of Jim Pendergast whose father, Mike, and an Uncle Thomas, or "T.J.," were the heads of one of the Democratic machine organizations in Kansas City. Through these men and others, Harry obtained the necessary backing to run in the Democratic primary for the office of county judge for the Eastern District of Jackson County.

Jackson County elected three judges, one from the rural Eastern District, one from Kansas City, and a presiding

Truman is shown here with his friend Jim Pendergast, whose father and uncle were the bosses of a Democratic party machine in Kansas City.

judge, who was elected by all the voters of the county. These were not judges in the traditional sense. The duties of Jackson County judges included the levying of taxes, planning public works, managing the county charitable institutions, and many other functions. They did not include presiding over a court of law.

Harry purchased an old Dodge roadster and made a vigorous campaign throughout the rural areas of Jackson County. He did some door-to-door canvassing and spoke at picnics and political meetings. Though he was not a particularly eloquent speaker, his straight-from-the-shoulder style was appreciated and understood by the rural voters.

It was during this campaign that Harry first came to grips with the Ku Klux Klan. Friends advised him that Klan support was necessary if he expected to win the election. At last Harry agreed to a meeting at a Kansas City hotel with the head Klansman of the area.

"Promise us that you won't give a Catholic a job," the man said.

With that Harry exploded. "I won't agree to anything like that!" With that, he stomped out of the meeting. When the votes were tallied on August 1, 1922, Harry had won the Democratic nomination by approximately 500 votes—without Klan support.

In November of 1922, Harry defeated the Republican candidate handily and in January of the following year stepped into his first elected office. He tackled the job with his usual enthusiasm and made an enviable record by cutting the county debt by some $700,000. The term was for two years and in 1924 he stood for re-election. This time, though, things were different.

A rival Democratic machine was still smarting at Truman's victory over their man two years before. Further-more, the Ku Klux Klan was fighting mad over Harry's snubbing. Nonetheless, Harry succeeded in winning the 1924 Democratic primary election. When November rolled around, however, his Democratic rivals joined forces with the Klan and the Republicans to assure his defeat. Harry lost by 867 votes. This was to be the only time in his life that Harry Truman lost an election.

Though 1924 was a sad year for Harry in the field of politics, it was a happy year for another reason. On February 17, Bess gave birth to a healthy baby girl in the family home on North Delaware Street. Both Harry and Bess were nearly forty years of age, but they were as excited about the event as twenty-year-olds. They even forgot to buy a crib for the baby. Mary Margaret, as she was named, spent her first few days in a dresser drawer.

As the year drew to a close, Harry was without a job. He still had his mind on politics, but knew he must wait for another opportunity to arise. He did not give up his political ambitions, which were to become presiding judge for the county, then a United States representative, then governor of Missouri, and, finally, a United States senator.

In the meantime he sold memberships in the Kansas City Automobile Club, a job which paid nearly double what he had made as a judge. He later went into banking, and then into the savings and loan business. He became a partner in the Community Savings and Loan Association of Independence. But the challenge of the political arena remained foremost in his mind.

In 1926, the Pendergast organization offered to support Truman for the office of presiding judge of Jackson County. This time, the rival Democrats offered no opposition in the primary and in the November election Harry won by a

margin of 16,000 votes over his Republican opponent. He was back in politics once more.

During Harry Truman's two four-year terms as presiding judge of Jackson County, many important programs were enacted. He pushed through a bond issue for new county roads and then proved that he would never be a machine "stooge" by letting contracts to the lowest bidder—regardless of political affiliation. Though he was a member of a political machine which was rapidly gaining a reputation of graft and corruption, Harry Truman drew increasing praise as an "extraordinarily honest" official.

In 1931, with the economic depression spreading rapidly across the country, Harry Truman, now in his second term of office, pushed through a major bond issue to provide for public works. Included in the package were plans for a new city hall, a new police building, playgrounds, a county hospital, new waterworks, and a new four-million-dollar county courthouse for Kansas City. This construction would provide employment for many of the jobless of Jackson County. By that time, the voters had faith in Judge Truman's proposals and passed the issue by a margin of four to one.

As his second term neared its end, Harry began thinking of his next step in politics. There seemed little to hope for. He was not really very close to "Boss" Pendergast and his chances of gaining organization support for a high office were slim. Pendergast had already named candidates for county collector, congressman, and governor.

In 1934, however, after three possible candidates had turned down Tom Pendergast's support, he offered Harry Truman machine support in the campaign for the office of United States senator.

In Europe that year, dictators Hitler and Mussolini were beginning to build up their armed forces for aggression. In England, only one voice—that of Winston Churchill, a member of Parliament—warned of events in Germany. In Russia, dictator Stalin was beginning his bloody purges to eliminate opposition to his tyranny. In America, Franklin Delano Roosevelt was waging a fight against the economic depression that gripped the country.

In that year of 1934, America was mainly concerned with defense of the western hemisphere. There were no commitments to European nations or Asian nations except the Philippines. Few Americans that year could have imagined the global commitments that would be honored by the United States less than two decades later. Few Americans had heard of the quiet man from Independence who decided to run that year for the office of United States senator from Missouri. Harry S. Truman himself could not have realized then that he would lead America to a position as leader of the free world.

Harry S. Truman in 1926. It was in this year that he got back into politics by being elected presiding judge of Jackson County by a margin of 16,000 votes over the Republican candidate.

The Senator from Missouri

On May 14, 1934, Harry Truman wrote a note in his memory book:

I am to make the most momentous announcement of my life. . . . I am a candidate for the United States Senate. If the Almighty God decides that I go there, I am going to pray as King Solomon did, for wisdom to do the job.

Almost from the start, the three-way Democratic primary race deteriorated into a mudslinging, no-holds-barred affair. A rival St. Louis machine sponsored Representative John J. Cochran, and Senator Bennett Champ Clark was supporting Jacob L. "Tuck" Milligan for the nomination. Truman, the underdog, worked hard during the campaign. "I made the fight," he reported as he returned to Independence on election day. "I traveled all over Missouri. I drove day after day in the heat and I feel better now than I did when the campaign began."

When all the votes were in and counted, Harry Truman had won with a plurality of some 40,000 votes. In the general election in November, Truman went on to defeat his Republican opponent, incumbent Senator Patterson, by some 262,000 votes. Harry S. Truman was now the junior senator from Missouri.

On December 27, Truman performed one of his final acts as presiding judge for Jackson County—the unveiling of the equestrian statue of Andrew Jackson at dedication ceremonies for the new county courthouse he had built in Kansas City. On January 3, 1935, he was sworn in as senator by Vice-President John Nance Garner. Truman rented the morning coat and striped trousers required for the occasion.

Bess and ten-year-old Margaret were left behind in Independence while Senator Truman searched out a place

Truman is shown here making a speech during his struggle for the Democratic nomination for United States Senator from Missouri.

to live in Washington, D.C. With the help of Victor Messall, who was to become his secretary and aide, the new senator at last found an inexpensive apartment just off Connecticut Avenue. It was a small place with two bedrooms, a kitchen, bath, dinette, and living room. This was the best Mr. Truman could afford since, unlike most other senators, he had to live on only his Senate salary. Next he purchased a few pieces of furniture on the installment plan and rented a piano from a music store. Bess, her mother, and Margaret arrived soon to settle in the apartment that was to be their home for the next ten years.

Senator Truman felt at a disadvantage among the other senators. Nearly all of them were college graduates. Many were former governors, lawyers, state political leaders, and big businessmen. Senator Hamilton Lewis of Illinois suspected that Truman was uncomfortable. He approached the new senator from Missouri one day and said, "Mr. Truman, don't start out with an inferiority complex. For the first six months you'll wonder how you got here. After that you'll wonder how the rest of us got here." Harry appreciated this good-natured advice.

There was a greater handicap to overcome than the lack of higher education. "I was under a cloud," Harry later admitted in reference to his association with the Pendergast machine. Many of his colleagues felt that Senator Truman owed his allegiance more to "Boss" Pendergast than to the people of Missouri. His Senate voting record during the coming months of debate and

legislation, however, disproved the myth that he was a "Pendergast office boy." His votes were cast solely on the basis of his conscience, the will of his constituents, and the programs of the Roosevelt administration.

Unknown to Harry Truman, Attorney General Homer S. Cummings was already conducting an investigation into past activities of Tom Pendergast and everyone connected with his political machine. Mr. Truman would not have worried if he had known of the investigation. He had a clear record and a clear conscience.

Senator Truman found his new job an exciting and interesting challenge. He especially enjoyed sitting on committees, and he was appointed to several. His service on the Senate Appropriations Committee gave him valuable insight into government operations and federal financing. He specialized in defense and military spending and enjoyed the interviews with top military and naval officials. He was a polite interrogator and directed his questions with quiet courtesy.

Senator Truman also served on the Printing Committee, which supervised the operations of the Government Printing Office. He was a member of the District Committee, which, in those days, served as a city government for the District of Columbia. He resigned from this committee, however, because he felt that the city was entitled to home rule.

There were other committees also, but the one which brought him the most fame was the Interstate Commerce Committee under the chairman-

Franklin Delano Roosevelt is shown campaigning in Wilkes-Barre, Pennsylvania, for re-election to a second term as president. Harry S. Truman was an avid supporter of Roosevelt's New Deal policies.

ship of Senator Burton K. Wheeler of Montana. Wheeler was a fiery westerner who enjoyed a good fight. He had a slashing, biting style which was quite different from that of the senator from Missouri. Late in 1936, Wheeler headed a subcommittee to investigate the financial management of railroads. He did not make Senator Truman a member of the committee at first, but noted his disappointment and permitted him to sit in on the hearings. Truman never missed a session and when one of the Democratic members resigned, Wheeler named Truman to replace him.

Then, in the spring of 1937, Wheeler and other members of the subcommittee became involved in proceedings elsewhere and Truman was elevated to vice-chairman. In the meantime, Senator Truman had been devoting much time to studying the railroads and learning something of the complex financial matters involved. By now he was virtually alone on the subcommittee, but proved to be a master investigator. His aim was to find the causes of the poor condition of the railroads and to introduce legislation that would protect the stockholders and also rejuvenate the industry.

As he organized his staff to go out and investigate the various lines, he soon found himself under pressure from lobbyists to call off the proceedings. But Harry Truman was not easily intimidated. The investigations went on week after week and month after month with Truman personally cross-examining many of the witnesses. By January of 1939, Truman felt he had sufficient

This illustration shows "Boss" Pendergast's arrest after the charges of graft and corruption in his Kansas City political machine were proven to be valid.

information. He brought to the Senate a report listing the reasons why new laws were required to regulate the finances of the railroads.

Senate action was slow in coming, and then the House of Representatives passed a different version of the bill. More months passed before a compromise was finally worked out and the bill was signed into law by President Roosevelt. It was known as the Transportation Act of 1940.

Principally because of his fair and thorough work on this bill, Harry Truman had acquired a somewhat better reputation than he had enjoyed when he arrived in 1934. The "Pendergast office boy" tag had fallen by the wayside. Meanwhile, the Pendergast machine had been destroyed forever. Investigation had proven the charges of graft and corruption within the organization. "Boss" Pendergast himself had been convicted and sent to Leavenworth prison. Eventually, 258 others were to receive sentences. But never was there a hint that Harry Truman was connected in any way with the crimes of the Pendergast machine.

Senator Truman's term was to expire in 1940, and early that year he began looking for support for re-election. Little was offered at first. With the Pendergast machine gone, many people felt that Truman had little chance of winning the Democratic primary. In January, Mr. Truman wrote to thirty friends asking them to meet him in St. Louis to discuss a second term. Only a handful showed up. Later, at a Democratic state convention in the same city, discouragingly few supporters came to call on Senator Truman.

But Vic Messall, Truman's chief aide, was undeterred. He began canvassing the state for support, and in February filed Truman's application in Jefferson City. Then Vic quit his job as the Senator's aide and devoted his time to being his campaign manager. Other

good friends flocked to the Truman banner, and soon the nucleus of a political organization was formed. Harry's old army pal, Harry Vaughan, became the campaign treasurer. Jim Pendergast, who had not shared the fate of his uncle, offered his support. Soon the railroad unions were siding with Truman, and despite a lack of campaign funds, his chances grew better every day.

Senators Carl Hatch of New Mexico, Alben Barkley of Kentucky, and the senior senator from Missouri, Bennett Clark, all came out from Washington to stump for their colleague. Still, the odds favored Truman's opponent, Governor Lloyd Stark, right up to primary election day. That night, Mr. Truman went to bed feeling he had been defeated. Early returns showed Stark well ahead. But with the morning came surprising news—Truman had won with a plurality of nearly 8000 votes.

On November 5, Senator Truman defeated his Republican adversary by nearly 45,000 votes and returned to Washington to begin a new six-year term. He had been elected a senator on his own merit. He had proven to all that he did not need the Pendergast machine.

Not long after his return to Washington, Senator Truman began getting reports of waste in defense contracts. By now America was stepping up its defense work as the war in Europe spread and worsened. England now stood alone as the rest of Europe lay beneath the heels of the dictators. In America, Selective Service had been enacted to draft men into the armed forces, which were being expanded rapidly.

To satisfy his curiosity and verify the reports of waste, Senator Truman made a 30,000 mile inspection tour of defense plants and camp construction sites. By the time he returned, he was convinced that something must be done. On February 10, 1941, he spoke in the

Senate Chamber about his findings and introduced Senate Resolution 71, calling for an investigation of the whole defense program.

"It won't do any good digging up dead horses after the war is over like the last time," he warned. "The thing to do is dig this stuff up now and correct it."

The Senate agreed and passed the resolution setting up the Truman Committee.

Truman sent out his investigators with these instructions: "You get the facts, that's all we want. Don't show anybody favors. We haven't any axes to grind, nor any sacred cows. This won't be a whitewash or a witch hunt."

Soon Truman and his staff were roaming the country, probing into the activities of shipyards, aircraft factories, mines, housing developments, and other defense installations. The Truman Committee quickly gained the reputation of being a watchdog against waste.

On December 7, 1941, Senator Truman was asleep in a hotel in Columbia, Missouri, when the telephone beside his bed awakened him. It was Bess calling from Washington, D.C., to tell him that the Japanese had just bombed Pearl Harbor. America was at war and the work of the Truman Committee was now more important than ever. Senator Truman hurried back to the capital.

As America geared up for the historic task of becoming the arsenal of democ-racy, the Truman Committee expanded its work. Senator Truman was now involved in endless hearings and frequent, long road trips. It was exhausting work and he reported to a friend, "I'm as tired as a dog and having the time of my life."

In January of 1942, Senator Truman read his first annual report to the Senate. With typical Trumanesque directness, he denounced the greed, inefficiency, and stupidity he had discovered in some parts of the defense program. "The fact that the entire future of the nation is at stake makes it imperative that there be a constant check to ascertain that the program is actually being carried out efficiently, economically, and fairly so that the necessary sacrifices are apportioned to all without favoritism," he concluded.

As the months rolled by, Senator Truman and his committee drew increasing praise from the nation. Americans everywhere were now aware of the great work of the committee, and as the year 1944 rolled around, there was increasing talk of Harry Truman as a presidential candidate. But Franklin D. Roosevelt decided to run for an unprecedented fourth term. At the Democratic convention in Chicago, therefore, the big problem was to find a vice-presidential candidate. When all the demonstrations, cheering, banner-waving, and balloting were over, the man chosen was the quiet senator from Missouri—Harry S. Truman.

Senator Truman first showed he was presidential material as chairman of a special Senate committee investigating the defense program. Here he discusses the October, 1941, sinking of the destroyer Reuben James _with Senator Tom Connally, chairman of the Senate Foreign Relations Committee._

A New Age—A New Era

When the Democratic National Convention nominated Harry S. Truman for vice-president, it had taken into account two facts. First, that President Roosevelt was almost surely the only candidate who could win the election for the Democrats, and second, that he was in very weak health and might not survive another four-year term in the strenuous office of president. The vice-presidential nominee was, in effect, the real candidate for president. Harry Truman knew this, too, but he prayed that such a situation would never arise.

The Republicans nominated Governor Thomas E. Dewey of New York for president and Governor John W. Bricker of Ohio for vice-president. After a slow start on election day, when early returns showed a Republican trend, the Democrats rallied to surge ahead. The final count was 432 electoral votes for the Democrats and only 99 for the Republicans. Franklin D. Roosevelt had been returned for an unprecedented fourth term and Harry S. Truman was now vice-president-elect. The two men were inaugurated on January 20, 1945.

Mr. Truman's term as vice-president lasted eighty-two days. During that time, President Roosevelt was in Washington fewer than thirty days, so there was little chance for Mr. Truman to familiarize himself with the myriad problems and tasks that would require his personal attention as president. What he lacked in information on that fateful twelfth of April in 1945, however, he made up in other areas. As a lifelong student of American history, the principles and beliefs on which America was founded had become a basic part of Harry Truman's political and personal philosophy.

Harry and Bess Truman campaigned hard during the 1944 presidential elections. Harry, who was the Democratic vice-presidential candidate, was uneasy because he knew that Roosevelt was in poor health and might not survive his fourth term as president.

With the initial shock of Mr. Roosevelt's death, Americans thought of little except their sorrow for the passing of a great leader and their sympathy for his family. After President Roosevelt was laid to rest at Hyde Park on April 15, Americans and the world turned to take a closer look at the new man in the White House. They found a dapper, jaunty man, nearly sixty-one years old, with steel gray hair, friendly hazel eyes behind the heavy glasses he wore, and a ready grin. Remembering the golden eloquence of Franklin Roosevelt, many were disappointed in the Missouri twang and plain language of President Truman. This very trait of speaking plainly and directly would, however, win the affection of the American public in the years ahead. There was a Lincolnesque quality about Harry Truman that appealed to the common man. His true greatness was concealed behind an exterior image of Mr. Everyday American.

Mr. Truman's first few days after assuming the presidency were crammed with briefings. Officials, military and civilian, brought the new President up-to-date on the situation at home and abroad. Edward Stettinius, the Secretary of State, explained the state of foreign relations. Military advisers General George C. Marshall, Army Chief of Staff; Admiral Ernest J. King, Chief of Naval Operations; Lieutenant General Barney Giles of the Army Air Corps; and Admiral William D. Leahy, Chief of Staff to the President; all offered their advice on existing war conditions and future military plans. Secretary of War Henry L. Stimson and Secretary of

the Navy James Forrestal also reported to the new President. Averell Harriman, Ambassador to the Soviet Union, flew in from Moscow to brief the President on Russian affairs. Fortunately, Harry S. Truman had a retentive memory and a sharp penetrating mind which could sort and develop a broad understanding of the vast data and information with which he was deluged.

Mr. Truman had his first face-to-face confrontation with the Russians on April 22 and 23 when Soviet Foreign Minister Molotov came to call. Though they were Allies during this war, the Russians were even then showing signs of the dishonesty and ruthless disregard for promises and treaties which would characterize their postwar attitudes and actions. Mr. Truman took Molotov to task for Soviet violations of the Yalta agreements. He spoke in the only way he knew—straight from the shoulder and to the point.

Events moved rapidly from those initial hectic days of Harry Truman's presidency. On the first day of May, Adolf Hitler committed suicide in his underground bunker in Berlin and his successors immediately began suing for peace. V-E Day, which marked the end of hostilities in Europe, came on May 8, 1945—Harry Truman's sixty-first birthday.

In July of 1945, Mr. Truman sailed for Europe and a meeting with Premier Stalin of Russia and Prime Minister Winston Churchill of Great Britain. This famous meeting took place in Potsdam, a city near Berlin. The new American Secretary of State, James F.

President Truman, surrounded by members of his Cabinet, reads the Japanese surrender message in his office on August 14, 1945. On Truman's left is his secretary of state, Cordell Hull.

Byrnes, British Foreign Secretary Anthony Eden, and Soviet Foreign Secretary Molotov also attended. The conference dealt largely with the occupation of Germany and postwar problems. An ultimatum for "unconditional surrender" was also sent to the Japanese.

Two incidents which were to have a significant effect upon the world occurred while the conference was in progress. A general election was held in England, and Winston Churchill and the Conservative Party were turned out of office. Mr. Clement Attlee, as head of the victorious Labour Party, became the new British prime minister.

More significant for the world, however, was the explosion at Alamogordo, New Mexico, of the first atomic bomb on July 16, 1945. Word was immediately flashed to President Truman in a secret code. "Babies satisfactorily born," it said. Winston Churchill had known about the atomic bomb project from the beginning because it had involved pooling the technical skills of both American and British scientists. When the President later mentioned to Stalin that we had a powerful new weapon, the Russian took no special interest and said simply that he hoped America would make "good use of it against the Japanese." The Atomic Age was born.

President Truman had already made the decision to drop the atomic bomb on an important military target.

On the first of August, the President left for home aboard the cruiser U.S.S. *Augusta*. On the sixth of August, Japan time, the first atomic bomb to be used as a military weapon burst over the Japanese city and military base of Hiroshima.

Mr. Truman was eating with the sailors in the crew's mess on the *Augusta* when he received a message telling of the bombing of Hiroshima. Turning to the group of sailors eating at the same table, he commented on the historical importance of what had happened.

Despite the terrible destruction wrought upon Hiroshima the Japanese still refused to surrender and on August 9, another atomic bomb was dropped on the city and naval base of Nagasaki. The next day, the Japanese Cabinet under Premier Suzuki offered to surrender, providing Emperor Hirohito could keep his throne. Allied terms were finally accepted on August 14, and a cease-fire went into effect. Two weeks later on V-J Day, September 2, 1945, General Douglas MacArthur directed the signing of the formal surrender of Japan aboard the U.S.S. *Missouri* in Tokyo Bay. World War II was over.

Truman, Churchill, and Stalin are shown here at the Potsdam Conference, held in July, 1945, to discuss problems that would arise after the war in Europe ended. The Japanese were also sent an ultimatum demanding "unconditional surrender."

In June, President Truman had witnessed the signing of the United Nations Charter in San Francisco. Later he addressed the final session of the conference. "You have created a great instrument for peace and security and human progress in the world," he said. "The world must now use it. . . . If any nation would keep security for itself, it must be ready and willing to share security with all. . . . It is the duty of powerful nations to assume the responsibility for leadership toward a world of peace."

Immediately following the broadcast of the surrender proceedings from Tokyo Bay, President Truman addressed the nation once again. "From this day we move forward," he said. "We move toward a new era of security at home. With the other United Nations we move toward a new and better world of peace and international goodwill and cooperation."

As America emerged from the darkness of the most terrible war in history, President Truman led his nation toward a new concept in foreign relations. Isolationism was dead. Henceforth, Americans would not sit complacently behind their ocean barriers. Instead, they would demonstrate an increasing interest and concern for the welfare, hopes, and dreams of all nations in all corners of the globe.

Truman addresses the closing session of the United Nations conference on June 26, 1945, after the charter of the new organization was signed by member nations.

Leader of the Free World

With the coming of peace in 1945, Americans hoped and prayed that war would never darken the world again. Nazism and Fascism were dead. Japan surely had learned its lesson. Now it was hoped that the Allies would cast away their war machines and work in harmony to rebuild a better world. But out of the smoke and ruin of World War II there emerged another threat to the freedom of mankind. The dreams of world conquest that lay shattered in the rubble of Berlin and Tokyo found a place within the Kremlin walls in Moscow.

American families wanted their boys brought home from overseas as soon as possible. In the first joyous flush of victory, Americans did not suspect the threat that lurked behind an iron curtain in Europe. But President Truman recognized the first signs of Russian intransigence as a very real danger. The draft was therefore continued and standing armies were maintained in Europe.

There were many domestic problems, as well, which confronted President Truman. Immediately following the end of the war, there was an insistent clamor to remove the wage and price controls

The position of the president of the United States as a world leader became very apparent when Molotov, the Soviet foreign minister, came to the United States to confront Truman at the conference table in April, 1945.

which had been imposed during the war. Men in business and industry wanted to raise prices but keep wages down. Farmers wanted to raise prices; housewives wanted them lowered. Labor union members wanted wage increases. The President, of course, could not satisfy the demands of all. Strikes by labor unions and lockouts by businesses threatened American economy and President Truman had to take stern measures to build a firm foundation for the postwar economy.

On September 6, just four days after V-J Day, President Truman sent a message to the Congress which listed twenty-one points of domestic legislation he felt were necessary for the nation. This message marked the beginning of the Truman "Fair Deal" program of "liberalism and progressivism which was to be the foundation of my administration." The program was broad in scope and concerned many problems, from equal opportunity for all races to reconversion from wartime to a peacetime economy; and from full-employment policies to demobilization. There was opposition from various quarters in the government, but the Fair Deal became President Truman's political philosophy throughout the remainder of his years in the White House.

The domestic issues seemed minor, however, in view of the foreign situation that confronted America. Russian attempts to influence the affairs of smaller nations continued. It became increasingly apparent that they were supporting communist terrorist activities in Greece with the hope of making Greece a communist nation. They were also threatening Turkey with demands for territory and control of the Dardanelles. Only an American show of force caused them to pull their troops out of oil-rich Iran. To President Truman, it was evident that the only thing the Russians understood was strength.

In March of 1947, the President asked Congress for $400,000,000 in military and economic aid for Greece and Turkey. The request, passed on March 22, marked a turning point in American foreign policy. History has recorded this new concept in American foreign relations as the "Truman Doctrine."

To the Congress and a nationwide radio audience, Mr. Truman said, "I believe that it must be the policy of the United States to support free peoples who are resisting attempted subjugation by armed minorities or by outside pressures."

Three weeks later he made another speech in which he said, "The world

Top, President Truman delivers his 1947 State of the Union address to a joint session of Congress. Seated behind him are (left) Senate President Pro Tempore Arthur H. Vandenberg and (right) Speaker of the House Joseph W. Martin, Jr. Bottom, Truman signs into law the $400,-000,000 foreign aid bill for Greece and Turkey. Looking on are members of the Cabinet and Congress.

In the photograph, President Truman (left) is shown greeting George Marshall, his secretary of state and the author of the Marshall Plan. In the illustration a Marshall Plan ship unloads its cargo of American goods which will be used by deprived European nations.

today looks to us for leadership. . . . The process of adapting ourselves to the new concept of world responsibility is naturally a difficult and painful one. The cost is necessarily great. But it is not our nature to shirk our obligations. . . . We are a people who not only cherish freedom and defend it, if need be with our lives, but we also recognize the right of other men and other nations to share it."

Meanwhile, Europe lay shattered, its cities in rubble, its industry in ruin, its economic life teetering on the brink of disaster. This condition was much to the liking of the Russians, who hoped to force communism on these stricken nations. Communism flourishes upon misery, poverty, and national discontent. It seemed only a matter of time before the Communists would force their way to power. But once more America stepped in to spoil the Communist plan with a program conceived under the free enterprise system. It was called the Marshall Plan.

General George C. Marshall, who had retired from the army, was named by President Truman to replace James Byrnes as secretary of state. His plan, which had the full support of the President, was to help the stricken nations of Europe regain their economic health. Instead of outright gifts or grants, however, the Marshall Plan called for the United States to lend assistance under a comprehensive program of helping these nations to help themselves. Not only was the program a shattering blow to Communist intentions, but it was also good business for the United States. With business booming again in Europe, America would have new markets and greater world trade would result.

President Harry Truman always made a point of taking a brisk, two-mile, "daily constitutional" walk every morning before beginning his presidential day. Secret Service men, assigned to protect the President, frequently had a difficult time keeping up with the fast-stepping ex-soldier.

One morning the President decided to walk across the Memorial Bridge over the Potomac River. Guards both preceded and followed him, looking everywhere for signs of danger. Halfway across the bridge, President Truman happened to pass an open door with a stairway just inside. In a flash of curiosity, he suddenly popped through the door and down the stairway.

The guards, who in that brief instant had missed his movement, suddenly realized the President had disappeared. Where had he gone? In a few moments, however, they came tumbling down the stairs to the bridge tender's room. There was Mr. Truman sitting on the floor talking politics with Mr. Charles Barnhill, the bridge tender, who was sharing his meal with the President.

Much of the love and affection that the American people feel for Harry Truman stems from his open friendliness to all—from queens and prime ministers to bridge tenders and farmers. In the words of Arthur Steinberg, "His is the story of the uncommon man whose blessing was that he considered himself the common man."

Stung by America's success in saving Europe from the clutches of communism, the Russians tried a new tack. On June 24, 1948, they clamped a total blockade on all land traffic between Berlin and West Germany. The former German capital, which is jointly administered by the Allies of World War II, lies deep inside Russian-controlled East Germany. President Truman was determined to prove to the world that America would continue to honor its commitments in the face of Communist threats. To send an armed convoy to fight its way through might well have led to a third world war. Instead, Mr. Truman directed that a giant airlift be used to supply the needs of the Berliners. This operation, known as the Berlin Airlift, lasted until May 12, 1949, when the Russians admitted defeat and reopened the land routes to Berlin.

The Airlift had demonstrated America's willingness to act when the freedom of a European country was threatened.

While the Berlin Airlift was in progress, President Truman ran for reelection against Thomas E. Dewey, the man President Roosevelt had defeated in 1944. As his running mate and vice-presidential candidate, Mr. Truman chose Senator Alben Barkley of Kentucky. Almost all the poll takers prophesied a Democratic defeat. Undeterred, Mr. Truman waged a strong campaign, covering some 22,000 miles on a whistle-stop tour during which he made 275 speeches to some fifteen million Americans. Never a good formal speaker, Mr. Truman was at his best when he could talk face-to-face with an audience. Americans admired his fighting spirit and his faculty for saying what he had to say in straight, down-to-earth terms that the man in the street could understand. When the votes were all in on election day, Harry S. Truman was returned to office with a total of 24,104,836 votes to 21,969,500 for Dewey. On his way back to Washington from Independence where he voted, Mr. Truman gleefully waved a copy of a newspaper which bore the premature headline, "Dewey Defeats Truman."

Meanwhile, the "cold war" continued as the free world under the leadership of the United States continued to resist Communist attempts at world domination. A major step in the cold war was the formation of the North Atlantic

Truman wins the 1948 presidential election by a small margin. Top, Truman holds an early edition of the Chicago Tribune with the erroneous headline "Dewey Defeats Truman." Bottom, Chief Justice Fred M. Vinson (left) administers the oath of office to President Harry S. Truman on January 20, 1949.

Treaty Organization consisting of the United States, Canada, Iceland, and nine western European countries. NATO was designed to present a unified front against Communist aggression in Europe. General Dwight D. Eisenhower was named Supreme Commander for the Allied Powers in Europe on December 18, 1949.

Mr. Truman had worked hard to contain the Russian threat in Europe. With his Truman Doctrine, the Marshall Plan, and NATO, Greece, Italy, Turkey, and Finland had been saved from Communist domination. In 1950 he made his Point Four Plan for technical and scientific aid to underdeveloped countries of the world. With this plan, America took the offensive in the fight against communism.

In June of 1950, the Communists took the desperate step of launching outright military aggression against the Republic of Korea. Surely, they thought, Americans would not bother to get deeply involved in a shooting war because of a few Orientals on the far side of the globe. They were wrong.

President Truman was in Independence when the call came from Secretary of State Dean Acheson telling of the invasion of South Korea by the Communists. He immediately flew to Washington and conferred with members of his cabinet and the military chiefs. In New York, the Security Council of the United Nations met in special session and called upon all members to render assistance. American troops, naval forces and air forces were immediately dispatched to the area.

President Truman believed that if the Communists were not opposed in the Republic of Korea, they would go on to other small countries in the area. Truman was afraid that this type of conquest would lead to a third world war.

At first the North Koreans drove rapidly through South Korea and the South Korean troops with their few American advisers were pushed back to a tiny coastal defensive position called the Pusan perimeter. General MacArthur, who had been named commander of the United States and United Nations forces, was rapidly amassing his strength, however, and on September 15, 1950, he launched an amphibious assault at Inchon. Soon the Communists were driven out of South Korea or captured and the United States forces continued to drive into North Korea.

Late in November, just when it seemed that complete victory was in sight, the Chinese Communists suddenly came to the aid of the North Koreans. Hundreds of thousands of Chinese, attacking in human waves without regard for casualties, struck the United Nations forces and sent them reeling back to the 38th parallel. Here General MacArthur stabilized his line, and here the battle seesawed back and forth until a truce settlement was reached in July of 1953. In the mean-

---

The war in Korea in 1950. The North Korean Communists had invaded South Korea and Truman reacted by sending American military forces as advisers to the South Koreans. Top, men of the First Marine Division ride amphibious tractors as they head for Inchon, Seoul's port city on the west coast of Korea, under General MacArthur's leadership. Bottom, American tanks fire on enemy troops in the hills of South Korea.

time, on April 11, 1951, President Truman had relieved General MacArthur of his command because, as the President stated, he was "unable to give his wholehearted support to the policies of the United States government and of the United Nations in matters pertaining to his official duties."

As the year 1952 rolled around with the fighting in Korea at a virtual stalemate, Americans wondered if President Truman would run for re-election. In March, Mr. Truman announced his decision. At a dinner in Washington, D.C., he said, "I shall not be a candidate for re-election. I have served my country long, and I think efficiently and honestly. I shall not accept renomination."

Despite pressures for him to reconsider, Mr. Truman would not change his mind. On January 20, 1953, he attended the inauguration of Dwight D. Eisenhower and left shortly thereafter for his home in Independence.

As "Mr. Citizen" Harry Truman rolled homeward on the train with Bess, he could reflect with great pride and satisfaction upon a rich and fulfilling career. From Missouri farmer, to artilleryman, to haberdasher, to machine

In 1952, Harry S. Truman decided not to run for another term as president. Top left, the Truman family smiles from the back of the train platform as they leave Washington, D.C. for their home in Independence, Missouri (shown at bottom left). Right, Truman enjoys a freedom he had been without for more than seven years by taking an early morning walk along a street in Independence.

politician, to United States senator, and finally to the highest office in the land, Harry Truman had followed his destiny with courage and simple dedication to the principles and beliefs he had learned as a boy in America's heartland. With an abiding faith in American ideals he had reshaped his nation's destiny and in the process brought new leadership and hope to the free world.

Harry Truman retired quietly with Bess to the old house at 219 North Delaware in Independence. Daughter Margaret, who for several years followed a singing career, married Clifton Daniel, now managing editor of the New York *Times*, in April, 1956. Harry and Bess became the proud grandparents of three fine boys—Clifton Truman Daniel, William Wallace Daniel, and Harrison Gates Daniel.

The photograph shows Mr. and Mrs. E. Clifton Daniel, Jr., posing outside Trinity Episcopal Church in Independence after their wedding on April 21, 1956. The bride is the former Margaret Truman, and the groom has since risen to be managing editor of the New York Times. In the illustration, Harry Truman's three grandchildren—Clifton Truman Daniel, William Wallace Daniel, and Harrison Gates Daniel—are shown with their grandfather.

In the presidential campaigns of 1952, 1956, and 1960 Mr. Truman worked hard for the Democratic candidates Adlai Stevenson and John F. Kennedy.

In 1957 the Harry S. Truman Library was dedicated in Independence, only a short walk from his home. This beautiful building houses Mr. Truman's personal papers plus those of many of his political associates. The library is operated by the National Archives and has become a famous institution for researchers of Mr. Truman and the other presidents whose papers are being microfilmed there.

Many high school classes come from all around the country to visit the library and view the displays commemorating Mr. Truman's political career which began there in Independence and ended in the White House.

And so the man from Missouri returned once more to the friends with whom he never lost touch during his years as leader of his country and the free world. The path of destiny had come full circle.

Harry S. Truman can relax as much as he likes (left) now that the burdens of politics are on someone else's shoulders. Top right, the Trumans visit the Churchills. Left to right: Churchill's daughters Mary and Sarah; Mrs. Truman; Sir Winston Churchill; Truman; Lady Churchill; Lord Beaverbrook, publisher of the Daily Express; *and Captain Christopher Soames, Mary's husband. Bottom right, Truman inspects a seven-foot model of the U.S.S. Missouri at the Truman Library in Independence.*

Summary

At the end of World War II, America had reached a crossroads in history—a crossroads it had met once before in the aftermath of World War I. In 1919, with its refusal to join the League of Nations, America had withdrawn once more from international affairs. In 1945, however, America took another road, one that would involve her in the welfare and the rights to life, liberty, and the pursuit of happiness of all mankind.

Something more than military security and political interests caused this change in American foreign policy. Americans were faced with the moral question of whether or not the richest, most powerful nation on earth could stand by while less fortunate peoples lived in economic poverty and famine or were swallowed up by Communist aggression. The answer, an emphatic "No," led to a new concept in American foreign relations and the emergence of the United States as the leader of the free world.

The problems of this new policy were immense and placed heavy demands on the courage and determination of the American people. To set the policy, to establish the precedents, to place America firmly and resolutely on this new road, required the leadership of a strong president. Destiny placed the reins of government at this crucial time in the hands of Harry S. Truman.

With a deep and unswerving belief in the American way, Harry Truman applied the principles of liberty, justice, and equality to international relations. With the Truman Doctrine of aid to Greece and Turkey, he demonstrated America's deep concern for the security of smaller nations. With the Marshall Plan for European Economic Recovery, he proved America's interest in the welfare of mankind. With the Berlin Airlift, he emphasized American courage and integrity in the face of threats, and in Korea he proved that aggression anywhere in the world would be met with force.

American policy was forever changed during Harry Truman's walk with destiny.

Bibliography

ABELS, JULES. *The Truman Scandals*. Chicago: Regency, 1956.

ACHESON, DEAN. *Sketches from Life of Men I Have Known*. New York: Harper, 1961.

ALLEN, ROBERT S. and WILLIAM V. SHANNON. *The Truman Merry-Go-Round*. New York: Vanguard, 1950.

ATTLEE, CLEMENT R. *As It Happened*. New York: Viking, 1954.

BARKLEY, ALBEN. *That Reminds Me*. New York: Doubleday, 1954.

BEARD, CHARLES. *The President In American History*. New York: Messner, 1965.

BERNSTEIN, BARTON. *The Truman Administration*. New York: Harper, 1966.

BOORSTIN, DANIEL J. *Genius of American Politics*. Chicago: University of Chicago Press, 1953.

BUSCH, NOEL F. *Adlai E. Stevenson*. New York: Farrar, Straus & Young, 1952.

CARR, ALBERT. *Truman, Stalin, and Peace*. New York: Doubleday, 1950.

CAVANAH, FRANCES. *Meet The Presidents*. Philadelphia: Macrae Smith, 1965.

CHURCHILL, SIR WINSTON. *Second World War*. 6 vols. Boston: Houghton Mifflin, 1948-1953.

CLEMENS, CYRIL, ed. *Truman Speaks*. New York: J. P. Didier, 1946.

COFFIN, TRIS. *Missouri Compromise*. New York: Little, 1947.

CONNALLY, TOM and ALFRED STEINBERG. *My Name is Tom Connally*. New York: Crowell, 1954.

DANIELS, JONATHAN. *The Man of Independence*. Philadelphia: Lippincott, 1950.

DAYTON, ELDOROUS L. *Give 'Em Hell, Harry*. New York: Devin, 1956.

DONOVAN, ROBERT J. *Eisenhower: The Inside Story*. New York: Harcourt, 1956.

DRUKS, HERBERT. *Harry S. Truman and the Russians*. New York: R. Speller, 1967.

DULLES, JOHN F. *War or Peace*. New York: Macmillan, 1950.

EISENHOWER, DWIGHT D. *Crusade In Europe*. New York: Doubleday, 1948.

FARLEY, JAMES. *Jim Farley's Story*. New York: Wittlesey House, 1948.

FORRESTAL, JAMES. *Forrestal Diaries*. New York: Viking, 1951.

GOLDMAN, ALEX, ed. *The Truman Wit*. New York: Citadel Press, 1966.

HELM, WILLIAM P. *Harry Truman*. New York: Duell, Sloan & Pearce, 1947.

HICKS, JOHN. *The American Nation*. Boston: Houghton Mifflin, 1949.

HILLMAN, WILLIAM, ed. *Mr. President*. New York: Farrar, Straus & Young, 1952.

HUNT, FRAZIER. *Untold Story of Douglas MacArthur*. New York: Devin, 1954.

ICKES, HAROLD. *Secret Diary*. 3 vols. New York: Simon & Schuster, 1953-54.

KOENIG, LOUIS W. *Truman Administration*. New York: New York University Press, 1956.

LEAHY, WILLIAM D. *I Was There*. New York: Whittlesey House, 1950.

LORD, RUSSELL. *The Wallaces of Iowa*. Boston: Houghton Mifflin, 1947.

McNAUGHTON, FRANK and WALTER HEYMEYER. *This Man Truman*. New York: McGraw-Hill, 1945.

———. *Harry Truman, President*. New York: McGraw-Hill, 1948.

MILLIGAN, MAURICE M. *Missouri Waltz*. New York: Scribner's, 1948.

MORGAN, JAMES. *Our Presidents*. New York: Macmillan, 1959.

PHILLIPS, CABELL. *The Truman Presidency*. New York: Macmillan, 1966.

REDDING, JOHN M. *Inside the Democratic Party*. Indianapolis: Bobbs-Merrill, 1958.

RICHBERG, DONALD. *My Hero*. New York: G. P. Putnam's, 1954.

RIGDOM, WILLIAM. *White House Sailor*. Garden City, New York: Doubleday, 1962.

ROVERE, RICHARD and ARTHUR SCHLESINGER, JR. *The General and the President*. New York: Farrar, Straus, 1951.

SHERWOOD, ROBERT E. *Roosevelt and Hopkins*. New York: Harper, 1950.

SMITH, IRA. *Dear Mr. President*. New York: Messner, 1949.

SMITH, MERRIMAN. *Thank You, Mr. President*. New York: Harper, 1946.

———. *A President is Many Men*. New York: Harper, 1948.

SPANIER, J. W. *The Truman-MacArthur Controversy*. New York: Norton, 1965.

STALIN, JOSEPH. *Correspondence With Roosevelt and Truman*. New York: G. P. Putnam's, 1961.

STEINBERG, ALFRED. *The Man From Missouri*. New York: G. P. Putnam's, 1961.

TRUMAN, HARRY S. *Year of Decision*. New York: Doubleday, 1955.

———. *Years of Trial and Hope*. New York: Doubleday, 1956.

———. *Mr. Citizen*. New York: Random House, 1960.

———. "They'll Never Make An Elder Statesman Out of Me." *Look* June 10, 1960.

TRUMAN, MARGARET. *Souvenirs*. New York: McGraw-Hill, 1956.

WEIZMANN, CHAIM. *Trial and Error*. New York: Schocken Books, 1966.

WHITE, WILLIAM ALLEN. *The Autobiography of William Allen White*. New York: Macmillan, 1946.

WOLFSON, VICTOR. *The Man Who Cared*. New York: Farrar, Straus & Giroux, 1966.

Index